Pre-natal Care for Fathers

Helping her down

Pre-natal Care for Fathers

By John Gould

With Decorations by

Martha Powell Setchell

———◆———

A non-medical, non-technical, non-scientific explanation of the masculine side of the matter, with much that is useful and nothing that is wholly useless

———◆———

THE SAME ADEQUATELY ILLUSTRATED AND DEVELOPED IN A MANNER THE READER WILL FIND HELPFUL AND ENGROSSING

———◆———

Down East Books

Down East Books

Published by Down East Books
An imprint of Globe Pequot
Trade division of The Rowman & Littlefield Publishing Group, Inc.
4501 Forbes Boulevard, Suite 200, Lanham, Maryland 20706
www.rowman.com

Unit A, Whitacre Mews, 26-34 Stannary Street, London SE11 4AB, United Kingdom

British Library Cataloguing-in-Publication Information available

Library of Congress Cataloging-in-Publication Data available

ISBN 978-1-6089-3536-9 (paperback)
ISBN 978-1-6089-3537-6 (e-book)

Inspired by My Son John

Foreword

REPORTS from the United States Bureau of the Census indicate a declining birth rate. In ten years the rate dropped from 20.7 births for every 1,000 persons to a mere 16.7. Men are not becoming fathers with the frequency they used to, and perhaps a lack of competent information on prenatal care for fathers has prevented many a man from plunging blithely into parenthood. Assuming that our breeding population is divided 50-50 between mothers and fathers, an assumption we may fairly make, we find that in one year approximately 2,144,790 potential fathers are in need of such information. What the figure will be in the future we have no way of knowing.* Medical science has made tremendous strides, and obstetrics has had its share of attention—but fatherhood remains uninformed and groping.

* We are unable to supply you with the data on the number of children to be born within the next ten years." —John Collinson, Acting Chief Statistician for Vital Statistics, Department of Commerce, Bureau of the Census, Washington.

. . . . *and played hideaby with my niece*

Introduction

ONCE upon a time I found myself doing little things that marked me definitely as a potential parent. I went down cellar and made a cradle. I began to notice small children for the first time in my life. I got down on the floor and played hide-a-bye with my niece. While privately I thought the whole thing was an old wive's tale, I refrained from dabbling in paint about the house. To my wife I became attentive all over again. I assisted her in and out of her bath, up and down stairs, and everywhere we went I held her clutchingly by one arm. I inquired regularly if she had taken her daily walk, and tuned up the bath scales that her morning weighing-in might be accurate.

The months passed, and each succeeding day found me mastering the apprentice problems of fatherhood. One thing I did was to buy my wife a fairly dull book entitled *Pre-Natal Care*. It had some revealing pictures in it but very little to amuse the wanton, and scarcely anything the wide-awake man hasn't at least heard about before.

9

The book served my wife well as her days were fulfilled, but it had not a particle, not a shred, of advice for the problems that confronted me. At that time it readily occurred to me that a book on prenatal care for fathers would fill a long-felt want.

The Good News

THE whimsical enjoy picturing the wife sewing on tiny garments, while the husband makes the obvious deduction with almost any sort of expression on his face. The husband, however, will seldom receive the good news in just this idyllic fashion. In most cases he will be sitting by the fire, puffing some fresh tobacco and thinking what a good year it has been for tomatoes, when his wife will address him in an unusual, far-away tone.

"Dear," she will say, "What day is today?"

He will reflect that today is Tuesday, the fourth, bringing his thoughts into focus after the manner of a man who has been thinking about tomatoes, and he will say, "The fourth."

She will ponder this to an extent that hardly

11

seems worth while, and he will drift back to tomatoes. Soon she will speak again. "Dear," she will say, "When were we at aunt Hattie's?"

He will reply that it was some time ago, and she will ask if he can't remember exactly. "Well," he will say, giving up the idea of trying to enjoy tomatoes, "It was the day Howard flew from Philadelphia." Next she will want to know if Howard had his vacation on the two first weeks or the two middle weeks of the month. "The first two." She will nod. She will stare vacantly at the rug for some space of time, and will say, "And today is the fourth?"

He will allow that today is still the fourth.

"Then," she will say, "Will you take me down tomorrow to see the doctor?"

Telling People

ONE of the first problems of pre-paternalism is that of telling people. The pleasures of connubiality are too recent for the husband and wife to divorce effect entirely from cause and they may hesitate to speak boldly. But there is no reason for keeping it a secret, because almost everyone, these days, knows how those things come about. Also, news will get out anyway, and you might as well have the fun of telling people yourself before they know it by hearsay. Anyone who is going to have a baby may be pardoned if he at first thinks it a quiet little homey matter strictly between the two in question. While this point of view is no doubt a hangover from Puritan ancestors who toned down the subject of ploughing, cropping, and reaping in the

. . . . *a quiet little homey matter strictly between the two in question*

human field, the facts are that whole communities relish greatly the latest news of who is having a baby. Anyone who cares to reflect will agree that the subject really has tremendous conversational possibilities. But even so, there are still people who shudder when the uninhibited bride yells across the back fence that her baby is coming in May. However, note well that while they shudder, they likewise thrill at the information.

So it is perhaps the best plan to inform those who are close enough to deserve the confidence as soon as possible.

It is generally considered inadvisable, however, to hurry too much in imparting this information. There is something pathetic in the picture of the earnest husband who has informed all his friends prematurely. A friend of mine, who fell into this unfortunate situation, was obliged to make amends at some speed, but when the baby was all of fourteen months in arriving we can readily understand why the husband's acquaintances chided him. Therefore, the husband will abide long enough to make sure, and will then tell as expeditiously as possible. The period of time in which the information can be imparted as a piece of genuine news is extremely short. Many alert neighbor women will jump at conclusions with surprising accuracy, and there are occasions when the husband will surmise that such news is not imparted at all, but is already dormant and comes to fullness by some kind of automotion. The wife, particularly, will experience side-walk chats wherein her friends accuse her of maternal tendencies even before she is sure of it herself. Many of these self-educated friends, however, are not intimate enough to warrant definite telling.

Maiden aunts must positively be told first. No one knows why maiden aunts derive so much fun from other people's having babies. They go around with a knowing smile, and gladden the whole countryside. Aunt Carrie has so much fun knowing what everyone else only surmises that the whole family gets a lift from her sunny disposition. While maiden aunts are noted for a tendency toward the unhappy, as related to the marital pleasures of the rest of the family, it is strangely true that frequent babies among nephews and nieces can keep them in fairly good spirits.

Brothers and sisters of the happy couple present no real problem. When sister Kathryn drops in on her way to the hairdressers, the husband can make some careless remark and take care of everything. "Well, it looks like rain, *aunt* Kate," he says, and aunt Kate nods with complete comprehension. It is perhaps true that brothers are less apt at these obscure hints. A fairly dull brother, however, should be able to understand something like, "Well, *uncle* Charlie, how are things at the saw-mill, old *uncle* Charlie, my boy, old *uncle* of mine?" If it takes more than that, there may be a tendency to think no unborn child should have such dense relationships cultivated further—but it is a fortunate child who has plenty of sympathetic relatives, and the husband should pursue the matter until uncle Charlie has caught on.

Other relatives, at some distance, can be informed in so many words by letter, a method that requires no special training. Here there is less likelihood they will feel hurt because you do not take them into immediate confidence—although this may not be true in every instance—but they will undoubtedly find it desirable to contribute baby garments, possibly a bit of cash, and at least their best wishes and advice. One of my most distant relatives, a half-great-uncle who lives among

We'd been on bats since time began

the natives on the Solomon Islands, was grateful enough for the information to sit down and cable ten pounds. This might not happen to every couple, but it is here significant because we didn't expect it to happen to us.

The prospective grandparents, if this is to be the first child, must be informed outright and immediately. The wife will take care of the two grandmothers in private—an act which requires tact in educating them to the fact that you, not they, are having the baby. Unless properly checked, grandmothers get the feeling that the baby is theirs, and only yours by accident of birth. The grandfathers can be eased into the information in any number of ways. A good method is to clap them on the back and cry, "Well, what do you want, a grandson or a granddaughter?" While this abrupt approach can sometimes knock ten years off the life of a sentimental old codger who has spent the past decade looking forward to grandchildren, it does the trick fairly well. Sometimes one can begin a bridge hand with, "What do you bid, Grandpappy?"

Intimate friends who are not relatives may present a problem. You have to tell them before they hear gossip, but they have a distasteful manner of receiving the news. With us it was the Kellys. Grace Kelly called up and wanted to go on a bat. We'd been on bats with the Kellys since time began, and when either couple made a suggestion the other jumped lively and we have a good many happy memories amongst the four of us. But now the doctor says to go to bed early and keep regular hours, and the Kellys are people who never heard of regular hours.

Thus arises the necessity of informing the Kellys there can be no bat. To say no and hang up is impossible. To say no to the Kellys entails reasons, and they'd better be good. The simple thing would be to tell Grace Kelly sweetly that Lucy is about to become a mother (*gravida est* was the way I expressed it) and cannot be roistering about the country as of old. I do not suggest this as a general procedure, however. It didn't work with Grace. She laughed fit to kill, leaving me defenseless on my end of the wire, then turned to her front room full of tipplers and bawled out, "Lucy's pregnant!"

I don't mean that Grace was unsympathetic, other things showed her keen interest and kindly devotion, but her manner of receiving the news was not a warming experience. Another time and another

"Whom do you suspect?"

place would have suited better, and I recommend some planning on this score.

In all. circles will be found a friend of the *ice man school* who receives the news calmly and asks, "Who do you suspect?" The coming parent can only waggle his head shyly and murmur something or other that never sounds at all smart. Probably every baby ever born was besmirched with a similar expressed or unexpressed innuendo and if the husband is caught without a comeback it may be redeeming to reflect that there really isn't any good answer.

After several months have passed there is no need to tell anyone. When your wife goes to club meeting in a smock, members will pick at it cozily and say, "Does this smock mean anything?" The wife will say yes, and the matter is then public property. Later people will gaze at her expanding facade and inquire, "Aren't you folks having a baby? I thought I'd heard something about it." It is proper then to say, "Oh—yes, I thought I'd told you. Didn't I tell you?" But generally, you may assume by this time that everyone knows.

Public Appearances

SHORTLY after the fact of conception is plainly appreciated, and retirement is in prospect, the wife will go through a frenzy of going-places-and-doing-things. The husband must discourage this as much as possible, in order to inure the lady to the days and weeks of static employment to come. However, a few public appearances do no harm, and it helps take her mind off the future. When people turn and stare at you as you take your wife to church or guide her into the movies, it is time for the lady to go into retirement. If little children on the street turn to their mothers and inquire, "Mummy, what's the matter with that lady?" you have waited overlong. Retirement is advised not so much because of your own or your wife's feelings, but because it makes people uneasy.

23

When people turn and stare it is time for the lady to go into retirement

"I thought she was going to have it right in my parlor!" someone will say if you go out to play bridge—even if the hospital is still two months away. This consideration, however, is for the feelings of others. On your own side of the ledger retirement allows you to avoid those kindly people who keep coming up to your wife to inquire, "How are you feeling, my dear?" These people operate under a curious kind of logic—their answer is the same and equally disturbing no matter what your wife says. It does the husband no good to hear them. If your wife says "I'm feeling wonderful," they say, "Well, just you wait, you'll not be saying that." If your wife says, "I haven't felt so very well," they'll say, "Well, just you wait, it isn't an instance to the way you *will* feel!" Avoiding these people is a much happier experience than coping with them.

Your wife will be encouraged to take daily walks, and so long as the husband is at the office the matter is of slight concern. On Sunday afternoons, however, the husband will go out with her, and a few words of caution will be in order. It is well to remember that the route you are traveling is strange to no one but yourself. The people along the way have seen your wife pass each afternoon, and now that she can no longer button her coat they know with some degree of accuracy why she keeps going by. On the first Sunday afternoon they will want to see the man of the house out of natural curiosity, but their interest is no reason for bowing at them and affecting a friendly attitude. The fact that they come to the windows is not, by itself, indicative of any esteem in which you are held.

You will refrain from clutching your wife as if the wind were about to blow her away. It is easy for a man to shower his wife with solicitude at this time, but recall again that she navigates this way daily without assistance, and will scarce seem to need it on Sunday. You are company, not a locomotive. There is something grotesque about the Sunday husband who assists his wife down the street as if he were holding a load of hay from tipping over.

It is well to take her arm. The husband will want to keep his chin up at such times, and not appear sheepish. Unquestionably there is a tendency to appear as the second fiddle. Women, at this time, assume a *savoir-faire* that always puzzles the men. They become most brazen about a matter that always seems, to the man, to have a smacking of the private about it. Women, most husbands will notice, are invariably more inclined to openness on such things; they will confer among themselves on matters that men would sooner keep from the general knowledge. But this appearance of strutting is an appearance only, and the physical should not be associated too closely with a mental attitude. Because she appears to strut, the man at her side must always appear to lag in enthusiasm. Obviously the gentleman will not try to make up for this discrepancy, as that will render him absurd in the eyes of the public. So the best method is to hold her arm lovingly, keep the head up, and appear to be taking a real interest in the objects one is passing.

Conspicuousness, during gestation, should be studiously avoided, and the proper time to cease public appearances will be obvious from various things that happen. In public places you will always run across those people who think the whole thing is amusing—young women hanging on the arms of sailors, and hearty mothers of fifteen or so children. High school girls sometimes giggle surreptitiously and young men on street corners occasionally leer with an accusing glance. Such experiences should not cause any loss of aplomb on your part, but when they become especially noticeable it is time to consider retiring your wife from public scrutiny.

The chivalry of well-meaning people is usually more bothersome than the amusement of the wanton. When a burly taxi driver squeals his cab to a halt, tips his hat solicitously, and allows your wife to cross the street ahead of him he is really acting from noble impulses. But his refinement is not due to any signal distinction on your part, it is merely evidence that goodness prevails in unexpected places. It is also evidence that your wife's condition is easily discernible—and it is probably time to withdraw to greater privacy.

Occasionally we read in the papers of ladies who were taken in public places. It was my good fortune once to be riding beside such a woman in an elevated train, and I can not stress too much the anxiety of the crowd in the car. To stand there looking the other way while the guard prayed for the next station was a harrowing experience. Anyone who has the least consideration for the feelings of others will go to any length to avoid such occasions. The well-informed husband will make certain that his wife, during the hanging-on period, will be con-

*It is merely evidence that goodness prevails
in unexpected places*

stantly close to some conveniently private chamber.

His thoughtfulness of his fellow-creatures will extend beyond the point of actual possibility. No matter how carefully the accouchement is dated, the general public does not know what you know, and the presence of a woman who inclines toward the looking-like-it is enough to set the nerves on edge. For that reason public appearances will ebb as time goes on, and toward the end of the period the husband will see to it that all contingencies are cared for, and the lady has no excuse for setting foot beyond her own door-yard.

Deciding the Sex

WHETHER to have a boy or a girl is not to be dismissed lightly—it will take several months to make up one's mind. Ordinary people, like ourselves, should decide to have a boy. Ordinary people, to look at them, would not be regarded as the potential parents of beautiful daughters. Seventeen or eighteen years later the hideously deformed infant girls have a startling way of blooming, but to look at their parents—people say—you'd never know it. Beautiful women, if mated to handsome young blades, ought to have girl babies. But ordinary people would do well to concentrate on boys. Boys are seldom pretty; they don't have to be. Boys can have freckles, and warts, and cow-licks, and ears stuck out—and they are still acceptable and very good little boys at that. There is, however, a sad lack of basic law regarding procreation. One can't just say to his wife, "There, that'll be a boy." But at least he can hope it will be a boy, and expect it to be a boy, and if it is a boy he'll feel as if he had something to do with it. If it turns out a girl, there is still the fact that no one had any way of knowing, anyhow. Some people predict a girl if they want a boy, and whatever comes is acceptable—they get the boy they wanted, or the girl they expected. Experience shows that most parents err in their desires, and the lesson from this is to want what you don't want, and want it so much you eventually get what you want. On second reading this will clear up considerably, and will simply demonstrate that a pretty good way is to hope for the thing least likely to please you. This palliates failure, and builds up an attitude of consummate accomplishment.

The subject of which sex to choose, since this cannot be settled prior to the nativity, would not seem to require much discussion in a pre-natal treatise; but the subject is probably the most important to be taken up. The budding mother is asked a thousand times what she wants, the father is beset with queries as to his desires. Both answer honestly—

an absurdity that passes without proportionate levity. If you want a boy they tell you not to set your heart on it too much, and if you want a girl they tell you not to set your heart on it too much.

No attention need be paid to theories that girl babies are conceived at certain times of the month, or that boy babies bulge more during incubation. First, you can't be sure; and secondly, no two women—to hear them tell it—ever bulged just alike. The woman now big with child is never quite as bad as her neighbor, who has a daughter four years old. "You're sylph-like compared to me—I was simply immense!" The present immensity is privately believed to be the worst thing the world ever saw, and the whole business is reduced to conversation between women. The bulge has no separate importance, it goes with pregnancy and that's all—like nausea and sore feet.

After you have made up your mind to a boy or a girl, the bulging may give you concern in another way. Some evening you may look at your wife and think, "What if it's twins!" There is nothing odious about twins. If they come along too soon they are sometimes facetiously accepted as an indication of exuberance following the wedding, but any physi-

Do not set your heart on it too much

cian will discredit this. The man who starts his family with twins should never be regarded as a powerful progenitor any more than he should be classed as lazy—and the chances are good that his next effort will be a girl weighing four and a quarter pounds. If twins come it will be wholly an accident, wholly unpredictable, and the odds against it. It is true, too, that occasionally the bulge will have this special significance—but if twins do come, there will be ample time after the birth to rush out and buy an extra set of diapers, bedding, and bellybands.

The best way is to plan for children one at a time, with a certain equivocation of mind as to the sex on each occasion. The husband has one priority in this connection: in the ordinary course of events he'll know which it is before his wife will.

Don't Get Chesty

A FEW cautionary remarks are in keeping at this time. Always bear in mind there is nothing wonderful about the fact that you are going to be a father. The bare facts of biological fecundity disprove that one does anything smart by producing children. Not only is the lowliest savage in the jungle just as likely to become a father as you are, but he frequently does, and exemplifies to us the proper attitude. For he, we understand, makes no association between the facts of intercourse and childbirth. People have had babies before, and people will have them in days to come. If your baby makes his mark in the world a brief note in his biography will record that he sprang from poor but honest parents—and that is your glory. Within your own small circle the little pink and white announcement cards will create a stir for a time, but only for a time.

Never put on airs about it. What you have done is nothing any man in town couldn't have done with half a chance, and probably would have done gladly. People dislike having you running around with your chest stuck out as an inference that you, and you alone, could ever do such a wonderful thing. Statistics on average birth weights show a lack of bragging material, and after you have boasted manfully for several months the perversity of fate will probably fix you up with a five pound daughter. Anything under seven pounds deserves acknowledgments, but no commendation; and your bragging will appear whimsical to the public. Seven pounds and over is worth some to-do, and at nine and ten pounds the father may be pardoned some advanced form of showing off. It is recorded that a woman in Massachusetts once presented her husband an eighteen-pound son, and we can scarcely wonder that the man forthwith went into the streets and in his excitement shot five people. This, however, is obviously an exception, and will not fall to the lot of every Tom, Dick, and Algernon. The

Do not be away from home when there is no need of it

point is that the birth alone will be the signal for jubilance, and until that time the husband will do better to keep his mouth shut.

Regard the coming child as a mere routine of life. The perfect husband will so much forget the approaching nativity that it will almost startle him. This will make him a favorite among those with whom he is in daily contact. Properly humble, he will not offer a rebuke, a challenge, a dare to his fellows. At the same time, guard against looking meek about it—head up, and look people squarely in the eye. One must be a little proud, or insinuations will be rife. And while proud, don't look too satisfied. There is a proper middle course for the well-behaved father-to-be—suitably pleased, sufficiently aware, sensibly gratified.

It is wise now, also, to point out that certain shortcomings may cause comment. Do not be away from home when there is no need of it. People love to watch and believe maybe something is up—another woman, no doubt, and his wife that way at home. But if you are above such silly gossip, there is the more important likelihood that your wife may think that very thing, and on slight provocation, too. Wives get very sensitive at that time.

If a man drops in and tries to sell you a motorboat, and you can't get away until five-ten whereas you usually make it by five, your wife is likely to meet you tearfully and ask, "Don't you love me this way?" Naturally you do, and no amount of coaxing and pleading by a span of wild mules would make you change your mind—but the feeble "Of course I do, dear," can sometimes sound like a left-handed vow. The careful husband will hit motorboat salesmen with bats and arrive home at four-forty-five as if the devil were after him.

The Covered Box

ONE of the reasons for telling everyone a baby is on the way is to prime them for gifts. All relatives and most friends will contribute some little knick-knack for the baby, and these presents go into the property box to await his or her arrival.

The size of the box depends on the number of relatives and your standing in the community. It is the infant's hope chest, and presents will arrive in various numbers until sometimes the parents hardly need to lay out much of anything themselves. The wife makes a practice of showing the accumulating contents to visitors, and this promotes further contributions. In a short time the box will have an assortment that depends on the local market or the handiwork of friends.

41

The father-to-be will probably find it difficult to get too much steamed up over this collection. It is good business to take an interest, however, and he can sometimes add a note here and there that contributes to the general effect. A box of dry-flies, an electric train, or a peen hammer not only introduces comic relief, but it serves to get the father really interested and with this leg-up he can help promote further gifts from time to time. The father will want to keep his mind on this useful aspect, because whatever is contributed is a penny saved— and if he can further the cause he is serving well at a time when little remains for him to do.

Occasionally the father-to-be can criticize and keep matters in hand. If women friends are running to lacy pink bonnets, he can bring an end to this frivolity by throwing in one of these white painter's hats the stores give away. Instantly their munificence is brought back to the practical, and the flow of useless pink lacy bonnets is stopped. For a real laugh the husband can toss in a box of cigars or a bottle of gin—although it is unlikely this sort of thing will be considered in good taste.

When a bundle comes for the box the husband is always asked for an expression of sentiment. He

Height and Weight of Men

Height.	Age. 15–24	Age. 25–29	Age. 30–34	Age. 35–39	Age. 40–44	Age. 45–49	Age. 50–54	Age. 55–59	Age. 60–64
	Pounds.	Pounds.	Pounds.	Pounds.	Pounds.	Pounds.	Pounds.	Pounds.	Pounds.
5 ft.	120	125	128	131	133	134	134	134	131
5 ft. 1 in.	122	126	129	131	134	136	136	136	134
5 ft. 2 in.	124	128	131	133	136	138	138	138	137
5 ft. 3 in.	127	131	134	136	139	141	141	141	140
5 ft. 4 in.	131	135	138	140	143	144	145	145	144
5 ft. 5 in.	134	138	141	143	146	147	149	149	148
5 ft. 6 in.	138	142	145	147	150	151	153	153	153
5 ft. 7 in.	142	147	150	152	155	156	158	158	158
5 ft. 8 in.	146	151	154	157	159	161	163	163	163
5 ft. 9 in.	150	155	159	162	164	166	167	168	168
5 ft. 10 in.	154	159	164	167	170	171	172	173	174
5 ft. 11 in.	159	164	169	173	175	177	177	178	180
6 ft.	165	170	175	179	180	183	182	183	185
6 ft. 1 in.	170	177	181	185	186	189	188	189	189
6 ft. 2 in.	176	184	188	192	194	196	194	194	192
6 ft. 3 in.	181	190	195	200	203	204	201	198	

must never say, "What is it?" He must say, "Sweet, isn't it, awfully nice of Sylvia." To himself he may confide that it's a horrid thing to wish on a defenseless, unborn baby, but outwardly he must show enthusiasm. He must only say, "Sweet, cute, darling—awfully nice of so-and-so."

The father-to-be is tempted to buy one of these pint-sized chamber mugs designed for the infant— a sort of apprentice jug on which he is to practice. This is not necessary, however, for at least a dozen will be donated before the infant arrives. Every time they give the wife a shower someone will wrap one in a big box. There is always one on the next Christmas tree. Former girl-friends of the husband frequently salute by sending pink and green ones with flowers painted on, all done up in gay tissue. If I were a young man starting out in business I would open a factory for making pint-sized chamber mugs. Millions of them must be sold annually to persons of frivolous humor whose friends are having babies.

One thing about baby clothes will strike the father-to-be as a thoughtful provision of the manufacturers. There is no sex to a diaper; no gender to a belly-band; no distinction among dresses and hats. If one had to wait for the baby before buying a set of boy-clothes or girl-clothes—the boxes would remain pretty empty. The husband will thank the manufacturers for keeping an eye to windward when the nativity finally comes and the box is so full the cover won't shut down.

Hankering

A TREATISE on pre-natal care for fathers must mention hankering—but hankering is something about which little can be advised. I was laboring with college English literature when I first came upon the subject. In some musty comedy I read a passage where two humorous gentlemen were contriving to learn if the lady of the piece were with child. Instead of going up to the lady in a straightforward manner and inquiring in businesslike fashion if she were *enceinte*, the two schemers repaired to a fruitery and purchased apricots, which they offered to the lady on a platter. While the theory was presumably well founded that a lady who ate apricots was with child, to my innocent scholasticism the scene was somewhat obscure. My professor, who was more anxious to elevate my knowledge than to explain such a delicate matter, came through in fine fashion by saying that women, while carrying children, are frequently vexed by unnatural appetites.

Since then, of course, I have learned that women are characterized by this sort of appetite at all times, but that pregnancy aggravates it. I am surprised now that there happened to be any apricots in England if apricots were that lady's particular hankering. The prospective father will find that his wife will want apricots only when the apricot market is at a dead low because of a seasonal lack of supply. He will find that she wants fresh strawberry ice cream in December and a thick roast of venison in May. In September she will want dandelion greens, and in dandelion greens season she will ask for big rosy MacIntosh apples right off the tree. In June she is likely to hanker for fresh pumpkin pie, and in pumpkin pie time she will want a tender brook trout. Hankering is a term that, when applied to pregnancy, means wanting something unavailable.

This would be bad enough if the matter could be dropped there. But the husband has the forlorn

47

task of trying to satisfy these simple tastes, and each husband will find the solution wholly up to himself, because no two women ever hanker just alike. Nothing I can say here will be of specific help, but a discussion may benefit husbands who are quick to figure things out for themselves.

Every woman waits in amused fashion to see what she will hanker for. At first she has no idea what it will be. Among our friends is a woman who craved pea-soup; another who wanted olives; a third who insisted on boiled lobster twice a week; one who ate positively tons of marshmallows between soda crackers; and another who couldn't get to sleep at night unless every window in the house were open—she craved fresh air.

This last might be considered a reasonable person until you learn that her baby was born in March and she tortured her patient husband through the rigors of a long, hard, northern Maine winter. The lady who wanted pea-soup afterward compared notes with the lady who wanted lobsters, and their husbands each thought the other's pasture a bit greener. One said he had spent so much money for lobsters that he'd like to see his next baby incubated on something as cheap as split peas. The

48

Among our friends is a woman who craved pea soup

other replied that things look differently to anyone who has been obliged to eat pea-soup six meals a week for seven months. The woman who wanted olives had her husband buy them by the gallon bottle and the store-keeper made a special price of $2.13 per gallon.* I have no detailed information about the marshmallows.

The hankering tendencies already mentioned are long-term desires and that sort will remain with the woman all during her time. Other hankerings may be classed as periodic or momentary—and possibly are a far greater problem. In the midst of Sunday church services she may suddenly want a bag of hot, fresh-roasted peanuts. She has not had hot, fresh-roasted peanuts in a 'coon's age, and this sudden desire in church will not be visited upon her again for some time to come. Or perhaps she will wake up in the middle of the night and want a ginger-ale float. Ginger-ale floats have not been her favorite refreshment, she scarcely ever took one, and after she has passed the present crisis she will wonder why she ever hankered for one. The husband will naturally make some effort to satisfy these whims. Sometimes a glass of orange juice

* In case lots.

50

will take the place of ginger-ale floats; sometimes a life-saver will do the work of hot, fresh-roasted peanuts. Then again, the husband may find it entirely within his ease to procure what is desired— a fortuitous bit of chance that hardly ever happens.

One friend whose wife hankered for double banana splits pursued a rather forward course. Whenever these moods struck her she was forthwith bundled into the family car and driven to the nearest soda fountain—where a double banana split was provided. The husband had a standing arrangement with the clerks, and instead of the customary double banana split the clerk would produce a made-to-order variety with a foundation of four ten cent scoops of ice-cream. Twice, during the period, the wife was taken to town after the closing hour, but the druggist was cooperative and came down in his pajamas to accommodate. The husband, naturally, figured that this method would place the lady in a conspicuous light, and would soon cause her to give over the whole silly business —but he was mistaken. Hankering is deeply seated, and it cannot be rationalized or ridiculed.

Another woman who happened to crave ice-cream (it was really pineapple ice-cream and no other kind would do) was unable to have her fancy satisfied. She lived far out in the country, and her husband wasn't going to hitch up the mare and drive to town for ice-cream. So the hankering for ice-cream grew on the poor woman while she jolly well got along without. Instead, she would go out in the yard and eat snow. This demonstrated that the desire for pineapple ice-cream was not so powerful that it precluded a substitute, and it demonstrated as well that one can't just laugh off a good hanker.

Other than to point out the tendencies and trends, there is no reason to pursue this interesting topic further at this time. If he understands the theory, each husband can apply it to whatever hankerings arise in his own family.

Inappetency

BY this time the studious husband will have observed that pre-natal matters hardly ever bear a relationship to anything else. The exception to the rule is hankering—like a geometry theorem it has a corollary. A pregnant woman always finds many things she does not like. Here, again, no one can tell what each woman will dislike, and no rules can be laid down here to guide the individual. We can only consider the general subject and leave the husband to his own devices if he cares to attempt a solution of inappetency problems.

My own wife hated knitting mittens. She likes to knit, ordinarily, and naturally figured that knitting would be a fine time-killer while she sprawled away her evenings. Just as she got into stride she found she couldn't abide the four steel needles used for mittens. Other needles were all right. But it so happened that all our relatives, who are a cold-handed bunch, looked to my wife for mittens. It was useless to plead—they got no mittens, and she turned out skirts and caps and sweaters and afghans until the wool shops loved her as a sister. As soon as the baby was born she was all right again.

My mother had an experience with John Mc-Cormack, the tenor. While carrying my brother she walked past a house where a phonograph was playing his recording of *Forgetting*. She instantly hated John McCormack, *Forgetting*, phonographs and the people who lived in that house. Mother has never got over that, although my brother is now twenty-three and has a moustache.*

Once when she was about to become a mother, a neighbor of ours took to hating the man next door. He was a dear soul, a puttery sort who raised lupins and begonias and whose unkindest act of a lifetime was to squirt nicotine-sulphate on aphids. This man would call a cheerful good morning to our neighbor whenever they were in their respective yards at the same time, and the lady got it into her

*A small moustache

head that he was making sport of her progressive bulging. She got to snapping replies at him, later would not speak at all, and finally actually snubbed him with a quick lift of the nose and a bit of a snort. The man was noticeably hurt and would duck into his shed when he saw our neighbor walk out. This assured her that he was not to be trusted and she worked herself into such a state that she began reaching over to pick his flowers, tossed her own weeds among his petunias, and shied pebbles at his cat. Before she called him names or set fire to his house she was fortunately taken down with labor pains and her baby boy took up her time from then on.

One very fine woman who married in her late thirties and came down almost immediately with a set of twins took to hating robins. She had previously taught school, had organized an Audubon Club, and used to lead her pupils on nature hikes. When the twins started along she couldn't bear a robin, swished her apron at them, called really nasty names, and heaved great stones. She knew it wasn't right, she tried to be nice to the birds—but she just hated robins.

Just to show the variety and the lack of uniformity among women, I have compiled a list of pregnancy hates. In the following list each item was disliked to the point of extremity by some woman who, otherwise, had no particular grudge against her respective item: sweet peas, telephones, the man who passes the collection plate at church, potted plants, cats, zippers, clocks with Westminster chimes, street-car conductors, letter carriers, whistling, goldfishes, the smell of fried onions, antimacassars, peanut-brittle, polka dots, flowered dinner sets, meter readers, dirty ash trays, lawn mowers, and the noon factory whistle.

Every husband can consider the inappetency of his own wife and add to this list. After recognizing her particular dislikes, he will observe there isn't much he can do about them. With a completely tolerant spirit he will accept whatever inconsistencies come his way, and the purpose here is merely to afford him understanding and sympathy—the two cardinal virtues of the model pre-natal father.

The Vigil

CONTRARY to the supposition of an unthinking public, it will be observed that up to this point the problems of prepaternalism do not touch upon the vigil—that dark hour when the husband hands his wife to the wonders of modern medical science and sits outside on an uncomfortable bench. Popular supposition has it that the vigil is the only time the husband can do with advice and attention. Popular supposition is still more incorrect when it thinks the moment is one of great humor. The greatest blot on the escutcheon of the medical profession is its failure to alleviate the suffering of the borning father. To illustrate the severity of this statement, let me erect an analogy:

I have hay fever and it is a nasty ailment. Organically I am fit. My wind is fine, my heart action is normal, I can chin myself, my alimentary tract functions beautifully. To the diagnostic physician I am sound and hearty—but I am not well. When I sneeze twenty-eight times in a row with the stamina of a whip-poor-will I am at once the most hale and the most miserable person on the street. I do not, however, get sympathy from my friends or relief from my practitioner. My distress is not even regarded seriously. People go out of their way to remind me that nothing ails me except I sneeze.

The impending-father pacing the waiting lounge of the hospital maternity division is similarly afflicted. Organically nothing ails him. Yet he is in unfathomable distress, with a distemper no disciple of Apollo has ever been able to probe. The old joke that Dr. Blake never lost a father yet is true through no virtue of the physician's prophylactic. The statement that women have the babies and men have the grief is funny only because people have the wrong attitude. While there is nembutal and sodium-amytal for the lady of the house, there is no spermaceti for what ails the husband. He suffers.

While medicine refuses to consider the case, I

. . . . just as I got my vigil under way

do know that psychology recognizes the mental, and therefore actual, existence of *sympathetic ailments*. These are much like sympathetic yawns after someone has evidenced boredom at a musicale. If you learn that a friend has an aching molar, it would not be unheard of if your teeth begin to ache violently. Appendicitis may rage through a whole family, but the first to report a pain is the only one to have any. The others are just sympathizing. Thus it is no joke when a husband has labor pains with his wife, as often happens, although the unthinking public is inclined to doubt. And on the whole the discomfort of the waiting-room-father is a real and present distemper that deserves more kindly attention than it gets.

As to suggested treatments for this distemper, I am not wholly competent to prescribe. My wife had what is known as an *easy time*. It was all over just as I got my vigil under way. After I took her to the hospital I went down to Louie's for refreshment, and returned to the hospital just as the doctor came hurrying out. He clapped on his hat, shook hands *en passant*, and drove out the ambulance exit very much as if he were on an urgent errand. The superintendent of nurses beamed at me and allowed

Sometimes a lady who has been rushed will languish in her room for several days

I must feel pretty good about it. She hurried down a corridor. Another nurse said my wife was now asleep and I mightn't see her until afternoon. Another volunteered he was the cutest thing they'd had in the nursery since the Holbrook twins. Thus I learned it was all over: no floor-pacing, no hat-wringing, no thumb-twiddling, no fingernail-chewing.

I find, now, that my friends' wives had *hard times*, a much more satisfactory thing to talk about. One let his wife have her baby at home, and she practically rioted. The details of that night have been told me many times, with a sneer. I listen ashamed, hardly feeling like a father at all, for while I do not wish my wife had been at it longer, I sometimes feel that life has not been as full for me as for others.

Although there is usually less need for rushing than the husband and wife suppose, you must rush your wife to the hospital. Occasionally this rushing is over-done; sometimes a lady who has been rushed will languish in her room for several days without anything to show for the quick trip, and sometimes they get up and dress and walk home to wait a few weeks. But at any proper display of activity, you will rush her to the hospital. You assist her up the steps and stand breathlessly before a uniform whose occupant seems to care nothing about anything one way or the other. She asks if you are Dr. So-and-so's patient, and you say you are. It is then proper to grin foolishly and correct matters by saying that, rather, your wife is. The nurse glares at you and pushes a button, when another nurse appears. Your wife is commanded, "Follow me, please." Your wife will be a mother before you see her again.

This little formula is varied somewhat if your baby is born at home. Upon suitable notification from your wife, you hurry to the telephone and call the doctor. With your heart thumping you hear a voice say, "Dr. So-and-so's office." When you ask for the doctor the voice says, "He is out at the moment, shall I have him call you?" Somehow this isn't just the way you expected it, but recall that the voice is not fully aware of what you have in mind. As far as the voice goes, you may be calling about Jackie Brown's green-apple stomach ache, about taking down the mumps sign at the Mc-Murtie's, or about making a fourth at a club party. You must remember that babies, to a doctor's office,

63

are in about the same category as Wheaties at a grocery store. Even when you tell the voice that your wife is taken it will display much less excitement than you will believe due. However, you will proceed to point out that your wife is about to culminate the period of pregnancy, and that for this reason it seems desirable to have the attendance of the physician. Nine times out of ten the voice will then say something like, "Well, he's in Millbridge to a lodge meeting, but if you think you will need him before eleven-thirty I can reach him." While subsequent events will undoubtedly disclose that you could have waited until three a.m., you will immediately say that you need him at once. The voice then promises to reach him, and you have only to wait. Up at Millbridge the members of the Masons, Odd Fellows, Knights of Pythias, or some similar organization will watch their brother arise in the midst of the exercises and depart—thinking how foolish it is for a physician to join a lodge when he is always getting called out. He will divest himself of whatever insignia he happens to be wearing and will leisurely get into his car and drive toward your place. A light burning in a home *en route* will induce him to stop to see how some patient is wearing away the evening, and in due time he will arrive at your home.

Meantime you have left the front-porch light burning, and have left the hall shade up so you can peer down the street for approaching automobiles every time you pace by the front door. Your wife, preferably in the care of some female relative or efficient neighbor, will have gone through a process of preparation beyond the comprehension of any proper husband. All you can do is heat water, and if you have faithfully attended to this task the kitchen will resemble a popular Turkish bath establishment during the busy part of the day. As the doctor drives up and stops out front you will of course throw open the door to facilitate his entrance. While your whole manner suggests a "Thank God you've come in time!" greeting, this will die on your lips as you see the doctor step from his car and get down on his knees to look under the bumper and see what has been rattling and banging so. However, he will come in before long, and after an initial examination in the bed-room upstairs he will come down to talk with you and perhaps play cribbage while your wife gets around to making up her mind.

While this indifference and unconcern on the part of nurses and doctors is a tantalizing incoherence at the moment, the husband should try to recall that the impending birth is, to him and his wife, fairly personal and immediate. To the profession, however, it is all in the day's work—and precipitate response by the doctor would be comparable to a hired man's running toward the bucksaw and the woodpile.

If your wife is at home, you can sit on the cellar stairs and wait, wondering joylessly what all the scuffling is about. If she is in the hospital, where all thoughtful men should take their wives in this day and age, you will retire to the reception room.

A society for the improvement of reception rooms in hospitals has occurred to many. Hospitals boast about their fine wards, their complete operating rooms, their X-ray and therapy departments. But reception rooms for prospective fathers get little attention. If they do get any attention, it is likely to be a poorly-thought-out program, like that in a New Jersey hospital where a friend of mine waited while his daughter was born. This hospital had been prolific—during its history an unusual number of patients had delivered themselves of triplets. It was almost as if the staff had power to beckon them. A newspaper got hold of the facts, and made a feature story of it. They sent a photographer around to find all the triplets, some of whom were now fifteen or twenty years old. All the triplets, from the old ones down to the new arrivals, were photographed with their happy mothers, and it made quite a story. The newspaper sent the original photographs to the hospital, where they were hung on the reception room walls. Each succeeding set of triplets was added as occasion arose. My friend waited in that room for news of his first-born. In an hour he was a sight. He finally fainted dead away, and was revived by a puzzled nurse who told him he was the father of a seven-pound daughter and everything was fine. He asked if there were any more to come, and the nurse told him in a matter-of-fact way that everyone asked that same question—"for some reason." How ill-advised that effort at improving the reception room was we can judge from the fact that my friend, whose daughter is now in college, occasionally rises in his sleep, and goes about counting, "One, two three; one, two, three, etc." I might add that his wife had an *easy time*.

I do not, however, suggest strongly that reception rooms be too well improved. For one reason, no one would pay any attention, and medicine has not progressed to the point where fathers are an obstetric consideration. But for a better reason, the father recovers from his vigil with a bound and likes to recall the horrors of the reception room in future conversations. It is like riding the *Whip* at the beach—it's a lot more fun after you've stopped, but somehow this retrospective pleasure does not immediately induce you to ride again. You do, however, stoutly recommend the *Whip* to anyone who asks you about it and you are delighted to describe the sensations. You would not, by any means, sponsor legislation to forbid *Whips*.

So instead of enjoying pool tables, games of darts, checkers, and similar possible reception room amusements, the waiting-father will divert himself otherwise. He does a little praying, of course, whether he believes in praying or not, and considers all the possibilities of this serious moment. He recalls statistics on the life-insurance blotter on his desk, but can't recall them exactly. He cheers himself by repeating formulae like: *This best of all possible worlds,* etc., or, *Obstetrics have made great strides in the past fifty years.* He should whistle gayly without making any noise. He recites, "Hope it's a boy but it won't be," or vice-versa. He checks himself at the recurrence of the *what-is-this-thing-I've-done* theme, and reflects in clammy awe at the power of generation. Any father-to-be who is conducting a proper vigil will find it necessary to allow ample time for expectant leaps to attention whenever a nurse goes by carrying a pan. Actually a nurse with a pan means nothing, but in your state-of-mind any possible bearer of tidings will win your notice. When they get around to it, someone will recall that you are still downstairs, and a nurse who will not be carrying a pan will come and tell you.

The practice of throwing one's arms about the nurse, kissing her smartly, and yelling "Whee!" arises from the sudden release of nervous tension, and not from strict social form or any regard for the young lady personally.

At this point the husband and father, if he pauses to analyze his emotions, will observe that the change in attitude is tremendous. A moment ago he was distressed, lonely, bereft. The recovery is instantaneous and complete.

69

For many years it has been a practice to pass out cigars when your child is born, and provision for this will be the last pre-natal care of the father-to-be. It is often possible to delegate this testimonial of your enthusiasm to the grandfathers, especially if the baby is a boy. In the event of a girl, it is less easy to get out of it—there will forever be something inapt in the prospect of a grandmother handing around the smokes.

DATE DUE

BRODART, CO.   Cat. No. 23-221

CPSIA information can be obtained
at www.ICGtesting.com
Printed in the USA
FFHW021247150419
51802010-57176FF